How To Be Found

SEO Beginner's Guide And Tips.
What Is It And How It Works, Engaging
With Social As A Marketing Tool

Celicia Lee

MP Publishing

Copyright

Table of Contents

INTRODUCTION 6

GETTING STARTED 8

SEARCH ENGINE...10

WHAT SEARCH ENGINE OPTIMIZATION IS. 13

*BONUS SEO SLANG COMMONLY USED...........................16

BENEFITS OF SEO AND WHY YOU SHOULD USE IT................18

KEYWORD RESEARCH...20

BEGINNER'S TIPS OF WHEN YOU CHOOSE KEYWORDS.......................20

ON-PAGE OPTIMIZATION 21

PAGE TITLES 21

THINGS TO REMEMBER WHEN CREATING TITLE TAGS: 22

DESCRIPTION META-TAG...22

THINGS TO REMEMBER WHEN CREATING DESCRIPTION TAGS: 23

URL STRUCTURE...25

THINGS TO REMEMBER WHEN CREATING YOUR URLS 26

WEBSITE NAVIGATION 27

HERE'S A SIMPLE EXAMPLE ON HOW WELL-ORGANIZED WEBSITE NAVIGATION WORKS: 27

FOOTER LINKS 29

HERE ONE EXAMPLE OF A FOOTER LINK FROM THE WEBSITE ZAPPOS. ..29

THINGS TO REMEMBER WHEN PLANNING YOUR URL STRUCTURE: 30

CONTENT 31

THINGS TO REMEMBER WHEN WRITING CONTENT: 34

OFF-PAGE OPTIMIZATION 35

TOOLS AND APPLICATION 38

GOOGLE WEBMASTER TOOLS 38

KEYWORD DENSITY 39

KEYWORD RESEARCH TOOL 41

BONUS TOPIC 41

BENEFITS OF WEB ANALYTICS 43

TRACK, ANALYZE, REPORT 47

WHAT PARAMETERS TO MEASURE? 48

VISITORS 50

KEY VISITORS STATISTICS: 51

WOOPRA 53

SUMMARY 56

SEO 56

WEB ANALYTICS 56

IN THIS BOOK YOU: 59

Introduction

Wireless access, rich media, pop-ups and pop-unders, streaming media, broadband, HTML, blogging, vlogging, bit torrents and more - these are only a few of the Internet-related terms that have entered the marketing vocabulary in recent years. But have you heard of Search Engine Optimization (SEO)?

Search engine optimization (SEO) maybe one of the most confusing terminology nowadays but the most talk-about aspects of people in the Online Marketing. What is SEO anyway? When did it start? And how it works?

SEO is a method of getting your web page/ web site on top of the list as possible on search engines. It is also a form of marketing used as technique and strategy to direct more visitors from search engines (such as Google, Yahoo, Bing, etc.) to marketing Web sites.

Looking back and tracing the history of SEO is kind of difficult to find on web since it is fairly young and changes frequently. Tentatively SEO began around 1995 right before hackers managed to cracked or get into first algorithms in 1997. That's when the time companies/business began thinking about placing advertisement and started obtaining ad space on related websites with links that connects back to their pages.

SEO is often used for online advertising as they called SEO = free advertising. Some may agree on this vision that it is free and some may not. But mainly, SEO is used for both branding and customer acquisition. It is an acquisition technique that is currently an explosive growth on the Internet which is also considered as the fastest growing marketing activity on the Web.

Getting started

Let's start by simply opening your browser and search for any product or anything that you want to buy or find in Google. When you hit search there will be search results display with the keyword / product that you entered on the search box.

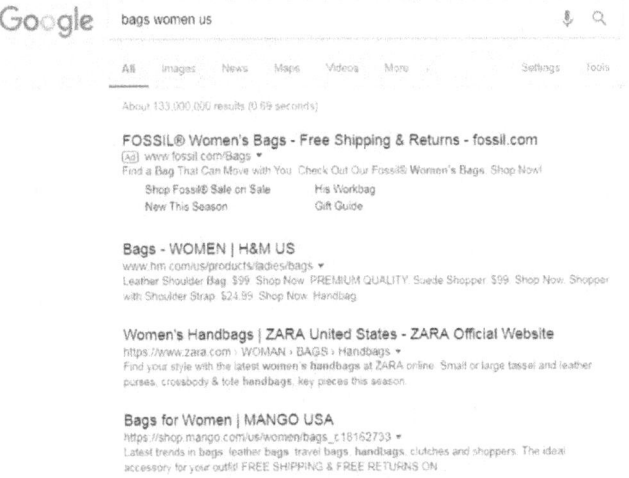

The picture above is an example of a result page from Google. Did you ask yourself how did Fossil and H&M make it to the top results page above all other websites?

Why are some words bold? And what are they? Is this what I am looking for? Which do I click and what do I do next?

All of these questions and more will be answered and discussed in this book. These questions were asked frequently by SEO beginners which will lead you on understanding SEO. The purpose of any website is to reach new, existing and current customers. The illustration above proves that the aim of any website is to be at the top of the page or somewhere on the first page at least on any search engines. There are two ways to help you achieve a high ranking in search engines, the organic (natural) and paid technique. Most online marketer says that there is no paid search tactic that will help you get a high ranking in a search engine, but using organic techniques will help you to optimize your website's content and improve your popularity/ranking with search engines to make your website visible to any online users.

Search Engine

A search engine like Google, Yahoo, MSN or Bing is a program that searches for and identifies from a specialized database based from the relevance to keywords or characters specified by the user.

Search engines nowadays seem to be overtaking their counterparts in many market sectors ranging from finding your old schoolmate to locating business services. Search engines, however, are the focus of attention since of their high ability to organize and make easier to access the vast amount of information on the Web. Like any other advertising technique using or getting to know how search engine works can also provide an advertising opportunity on many website owners. To think of how they do this is highly technical and ever-changing.

There are three basic components of a search engine. All search engines have a crawler, some may be referred to as spider or robots. As search engines crawl websites, they use special mathematical formulas called search algorithms, which helps to organize, file and rank information in order of relevance to a particular search keyword. As it moves from one link to another it finds pages and sends them back to the search engine index. The index is a massive database that organizes Web content according to its own criteria. With any criteria it uses, the goal is to produce relevant data for keyword search. How relevant data show based on keyword search? Imagine a database of books, when someone searches the database for "Anatomy of the Heart", all relevant publications appear in the search results. The third piece of the search engine is a query processor that takes the words typed into the search box, transmits it to the index and returns a search engine result page to the user. The value, and therefore the popularity, of the search engine, is determined by the relevance of those results.

The issue with most of the websites is that they are not search engine "friendly". One is Google for example, it may not be able to find the "title" or "description" of your site, links could be broken, pages might not be landed correctly and your navigation may not optimized for search engine crawlers (spiders/ bots). This is where Search Engine Optimization plays a role. By making small modifications to parts of your website, your website's user/visitor experience and performance in organic search results may increase dramatically.

What Search Engine Optimization is.

The term Search Engine Optimization was coined in the mid-early 1990's when search providers like Ask.com and Lycos were started but promptly evolved since the arrival of Google. Looking back and tracing the history of SEO is kind of difficult to find on the web since it is fairly young and changes frequently. SEO had no structure; people just simply added popular and commonly used keywords to the meta-tags of a site, whether they were unrelated to the contents of the website.

At the early stage of SEO people went overboard and abused SEO tactics. Keyword stuffing was extensive that time, since adding keywords to meta-data and selecting keywords to optimized content on website is legal. Websites were submitted to thousands of search engines resulting rank you higher in search results. There were many HTML tricks discovered to hide text and boost keywords density, these tricks/scams were not detected by

SEO as it is not refined enough so websites got high rankings very quickly.

Finally, in the early 21st century, Google arrived in the market and changed the rule of SEO radically by introducing the idea of backlinks to rank a website. Backlink basically is incoming links to a web page. It is the process of when a webpage links to another page. It became a major metric for the ranking of a webpage, rather than simply analyzing the content on a webpage, which is far easier to handle. The concept of analyzing the website's backlink started when Google developed their link algorithm called PageRank. PageRank works by measuring the importance and relevance of website pages in terms of the number of external websites that link back to it.

Today, SEO has moved rapidly to a new era of sophistication. The SEO now process involves processing large quantities of data, mathematical calculations, algorithms, analysis and regular monitoring of websites for their relative keywords. It contributes a huge role from small-business owner to a professional marketer to understand the essential tasks of search engine optimization. This will not only help achieve higher ranking on search engines but also monitor competition and make small modifications to your website that will increase or stay your search rankings.

*bonus SEO Slang commonly used

Search engine marketing (SEM)- a set of techniques and strategies used to direct more visitors from search engines to your own websites. Includes paid and natural (organic) search engine activities.

Organic Search – also referred as natural search is a method used to obtain high placement or ranking on search engines in an unpaid algorithm-driven result. Usually ranked by relevance based on the keyword or phrase chosen.

Paid Search – is the opposite complex of organic search. It is set up to be easy for the average marketer to place an ad search engines to achieve a high ranking.

Meta-tags- HTML code that describes the website to a search engine. Search engines use the content of these tags to help them organize websites in order of relevance to a particular query.

17

Keywords- Specific terms used to search for something on the internet. Some keywords are more popular than others and will generate more search engine results.

Keyword Stuffing- filling a webpage with keywords in an attempt to manipulate a site's ranking in search engine results. An example is to mention the same word or variations of it many times in the meta-description for a website or even in hidden places on the page itself.

Benefits of SEO and why you should use it.

Easy navigation on your website – SEO help website owners to create a faster, smoother and user-friendly website. SEO today is also about improving user experience too. By providing a well-structured, clean and organized websites lead the visitors to stay longer on your website. Likewise, bringing highly relevant content and articles like blogs, sale pages, and reviews keeps your visitors happy as it helps them to find exactly what they're looking for on your website.

Bring in more customers- 85% of internet users find websites through search engines similarly the intention of users to purchase product or service by search engines is high. It is also said that 90% of the internet users do not to go past the top 30 search results (10 results per page). A good SEO website brings more targeted customers to your website and converting visitors to customers is one of the essential goals of SEO. The more targeted traffic (visitors) equals more sales.

Build Brand Awareness- SEO helps build an online brand presence and long-term positioning. You're your sites appear on the first page of major engines like Google, Bing, Yahoo!, your potential customers are more likely to trust in your brand. Search engine rankings are relatively stable compared to PPC (Pay-Per-Click) and cheaper but work over a longer term than other marketing strategies.

Return on Investment (ROI) - SEO has a better ROI than any other marketing medium. The only cost spent on SEO is the time spent on researching, gathering, calculating and analyzing data. It is also known as non-biased since SEO only generate natural (organic) listing. It is said that natural listings convert 30% more than paid listings and the percentage of clicks on organic search increase with the level of education of online users.

Keyword Research

Keywords are the specific terms used to search for something on the internet. More popular keywords is more likely generate more search engine results. Keywords are commonly used on the written content of your site, page titles, meta-data and the structure of your URL.

Beginner's tips of when you choose keywords

Always choose keywords that are relevant to your website's content.

Make sure that you have enough related content in which to integrate the keywords you've chosen.

Always check your competitors and list their names and URLs.

You can also right click on the home page of each competitor and select the "View source" option from the list that appears. You will be able to view their page title, meta-description and keywords.

On-page Optimization

As SEO is all about putting your website on top of the list in search engines, there is still a variety of on-page optimization technique that can be applied to your site in order to increase search engine rankings and resulting traffic. The following principles below should always be applied to ensure better optimization.

Page Titles

A title tag tells both users and search engines what the topic of a particular page is. The title should be placed inside <title></title> tags within the header section of the HTML document.

When creating a unique title for each page makes sure that it is closely matches the content of that web page. You can also view competitors HTML information by going to their home page and right click to view source. By pressing Ctrl + F and enter "Title" you will be able to find the exact title of that page.

Things to remember when creating title tags:

- Always describe the content of the web page. Search engines more likely to find a match between titles and contents.

- Unique titles on your lower-level pages on your website must still have title tags to describe the content of your particular pages.

- Get to the point. Using the first 65 characters of a title tag is more likely indexes by Google. Make sure the length of the title is shorter as Google assigns more emphasis to words at the beginning of the tag than the end, so it is important to put your keywords at the beginning.

- Don't stuff keywords. Make sure your title tag is informative but still readable. There are still users that will be reading tags in result pages, so its contents also influence the users whether they'll click through on your listing or not.

Description meta-tag

Descriptions are usually sentences or short paragraphs on the content of a web page. Page description meta-tag gives search engines a summary of what the page is about. One of the tools used to analyze whether your description and title tags are too long, too short or duplicated. Google Webmaster tools is one of them, though meta-description tags are not used in Google's algorithm to get a higher rank page, it is still important to get your content shown in the search engine results.

Things to remember when creating description tags:

• Summarize or make a short paragraph of your page content in the description tag. Example (<head>

<title>Bags and Shoes Women – b&swomen.com </title>

<meta name="description" content="The leading retailer of bags & shoes for women at surprisingly affordable prices, in a wide variety of on-trend styles!/>

</head>>

• Try to write a unique description for each page but always make sure that description tags are relevant to the content of the page.

- Do not fill description page with just keywords; try to write an informative sentence as other readers more likely to trust it.

(Keyword meta-tags maybe sound familiar to you; it works the same as description meta-tag but a shorter version. It is also a tag that sits in the <head> tag and lists any keywords related to the website. Although key meta-tagging has a little value in keyword tags due to the prevalence of keyword stuffing, it is still a good practice to include these tags on every page of your website. This can be useful once the search engine cannot find any other content present on the page that can tell the search engine what the web page it is about. One case is when a page only contains images with no text. Here's an example of Bags & Shoes Women keyword meta-tags:

<meta name="keywords" content="bags, shoes, women, fashion, online shopping, united states, usa" />)

URL Structure

Uniform Structure Locator also is known as (URL) is the unique location or address for your website and all the files, documents, and images that make it up. For example b&swomen.com is the global address of Bags & Shoes Women not just for the home page but for all lower-level pages. As mentioned search engines crawl your website looking for valuable information so it is important to be able to read a file, page, image or document in order to index it accordingly. Having a good URL structure will help you to have Google assign a large amount of relevance to a page and search query if the keyword in that query is existing in URL. For example, below is an example of poorly structured URL for SEO:

•

www.b&swomen.com/about/12145c7a/1882t28/79q.html

As one of the internet users, this URL is not easy remember same as Google will not be able to read and cannot pick relevant keywords.

Here are two examples of well-structured URL's for SEO.

- www.b&swomen.com/about/directories/contact-numbers

- www.b&swomen.com/about/branches/maps/brooklyn-new-york.html

Having a well-structured URL will be easier for users to know where they are on your website and what page they are currently on, while Google knows that the first URL is likely to contain information about "Contact Numbers", while the second URL is likely to be about "Brooklyn New York branch". So imagine when someone searches for that particular contact number or location, it will, therefore, have a better chance of appearing in related search results if the URL is well-structured and has keywords relevant to the content of the page.

Things to remember when creating your URLs

- Always use keywords in the URL that are relevant to the content of that particular page.
- Keep URL's short and unique.

- Have a simple structure on your site so that users can find their way easily. (e.g home > shoes > boots).

- Only use one version of a URL to reach a particular page, avoid multiple versions like having a content that already exists from a different page.

Website Navigation

Website navigation works like how you organize your files in your computer. For example, instead of having a thousand of pictures under "Desktop", you could organize your pictures by date or event (e.g 2001 Xmas, 2005 Xmas, 2015 Xmas) and place them into folder accordingly. Websites operate in the same way too. A well-organized site helps visitors move between pages in a seamless manner. All website a have a landing page, which is usually the home page. Usually, the home page is "call-to-action" part of your website where it links the visitors to the lower-level pages with more specific content on a particular topic.

Here's a simple example on how well-organized website navigation works:

1. Home

   www.b&swomen.com

2. Bags

   www.b&swomen.com/bags/index.php

   All

   www.b&swomen.com/bags

   Styles

   www.b&swomen.com/bags/styles

   Backpacks

   www.b&swomen.com/bags/styles/back-packs

   Sling bags

   www.b&swomen.com/bags/styles/sling-bags

   Shoulder Leather

   www.b&swomen.com/bags/styles/shoulder-leather

3. For Kids

   www.b&swomen.com/bags/kids

From the example, you will notice that the URL structure reflects the navigation of the website. As visitors click all throughout, the URL moves deeper into a file structure.

You can go ahead and try looking other website's structure and you will notice that not all websites take up this as best practice rule of site navigation. It is more likely advantageous that the more organized you are at the start of your web page; the easier it will be to manage when site added more pages.

Footer Links

Another way for users and search engines to find content is through text links on the site, which are often located in the footer of the website. Footer links are typically "shortcuts" to key content areas that already exist in the site's home navigation. Footer links are important as well because search engines often can't obtain context from navigational menu links, since they're typically contained within graphics or JavaScript rather than in plain text. The footer should be a "global footer" on all pages of a website, which means it should appear on all your web pages.

Here one example of a footer link from the website Zappos.

Explore Zappos	Customer Service	About Zappos
Brands	FAQs	About
Clothing	Contact Info	Zappos for Good
Luxury	¿Ayuda en español?	Jobs
Eyewear	Shipping And Returns	Press Kit
New Arrivals	Safe Shopping Guarantee	Tours
Outdoor	Secure Shopping	Customer Testimonials
Rideshop		Associates Program
Running	**Fit Info**	Glossary of Terms
Shoes	Measurement Guide	Site Map
Watches	Model Measurements	
Wedding	Size Conversion Chart	**Feedback**
Zappos Adaptive	Measure Your Bra Size	How do you like our
All Departments		website?

As you noticed Zappos has highlighted their product categories, customer service, also fit info. When planning your footer links, make sure that it is in an HTML text for and not images. As Google can find these as keywords when users search through search engines.

Things to remember when planning your URL structure:

• Keep it natural and user-friendly. Users should be able to navigate on your website thoroughly to find content without searching.

• Using mainly text when creating navigation is more likely easier for both users and search engines to find pages and relevant information.

31

Avoid using numbers or random characters that is not relevant and may be confusing for search engines and your visitors.

- Creating an Error 404 page that appears on your page if the page you are looking for does not exist, or the link broken is also recommended. So that visitors are guided back to your website and will be advised that they happen to land on a non-existent page. To make it possible, you can ask your IT or technical team to setup a custom 404 pages and make sure they are not indexed by search engine.

Content

Writing an interesting and compelling content is the one of most important part of your website, especially for visitor retention and search engine crawling. Once you finalize your keyword list, make sure that you integrate these keywords into the meta-tags, heading, and content of each page in a relevant and informative manner. Having the right keywords should appear in your copy naturally without too much effort. Keep in mind that the content of your webpage is for readers too, you have to balance your content or writing between SEO and readability. With a good-quality content, it spreads from user to user really quick as it has a big impact because people like to share valuable information. This is also referred as word of mouth buzz, and it usually happens on a blog post when a blogger finds some interesting content on your website and write about it and then link to your website. Blogs, social media and email campaigns that point all to your website and search engines make the connection between similar types of content, links, and keywords that can be critical for SEO. In order to maintain your SEO structure it is important to be consistent in the quality of your writing and keyword density across all marketing initiatives, whether it is on or offline.

- Anchor Text – is the clickable text that users see as a result of a link and placed within an anchor tag <a href="..."> </a>. Search engine are more likely to assign relevance to the keywords contained within the anchor tag to the destination page. It is important to be as specific as possible when creating an anchor text so that users will be able to see which destination they will be going once they click it.

- Headings- are also one of the important content element on a web page. Heading tags usually make the text bigger and have different sizes. If you are familiar with HTML coding <h1> is the biggest and <h8> is the smallest and least important. Search engines are likely to read headings in order of importance. All page headings should be <h1>, large and bold that makes it easier for the user to and read the body copy and stand out. It is always recommended to use one <h1> tag per page to prioritize the content. Having also consistent with the heading tag sizes and styles across your website helps define the well-structured webpage. Lastly, make sure you use heading tags and not images or image text for headings as the search engine will not be able to read it.

- Images- having a high-quality flash and images are fantastic ways to make a website appealing and compelling to readers. However, search engines have difficulty on reading the content contained within Flash files and also not all users have the capability to download Flash elements. Images may be easier for web owners to show a straightforward component of a website. You can still use Flash elements by optimizing it within the HTML page. Remember the analogy of the file system; where all images can have a distinct file name and an "alt" attribute. The "alt" attribute will allow you to specify alternative text for the image if it cannot be displayed for any reason. This will help provide search engines with context about that image you may also add keywords to your "alt" tags, as long as they are relevant to your image. Lastly, make sure you use unique file names for all images, and not generic names like image1.jpg, image2.jpg, etc.

Things to remember when writing content:

- Make a list of all the words you would use to search content on your website. Refer back to your keyword research and look for top search queries that your site appears for and the ones that led the most users to your website. You can use Google Webmasters to guide. (https://www.google.com/webmasters/learn/)

- Never write a duplicate copy, as it won't help gain search engine visibility and will leave bad user experience to your visitors who will be shown with multiple versions of the same content.

- Always write for readability for your readers and not for search engines.

- First paragraph is the most critical part of SEO; make sure your title and description tags are also in the first paragraph of your copy.
- Meta-tags should be always at the very top of the HTML code inside the head tags as search engines are more likely to read it first.

Off-page optimization

As previously mentioned earlier in this book, one of the main ways in which Google assigns a value to one page to another is by analyzing the quality and quantity of links pointing to a particular page. There are lots of ways to increase the number of good-quality links that point to your site. These include by seeking links from sites that you already have an existing business with whether it's a customer or a vendor, distributing content that links back to your site, and submitting your site to related directories.

- Partner linking- asking your business partners, customers, clients, vendors, or suppliers to link back to your site under their "resources section" in order to add value and visibility to their own visitors.

- Content distribution- is when you submit your content and articles to distributors who publish content across the content networks. When submitting always make sure to include a link back to your site at the end of the piece of content. This will help increase exposure about your company that can lead to increase your traffic and brand awareness.

- Open source and business directories- add your website to network directories like DMOZ as well as local business directories. You can use Google's local business center for free (www.google.com/local/add).

- Blog indexing- submitting your company blog to blog directories creates an inbound link back to your site as long as your blog is contained on the same domain as your website, which then impacts your site's search rankings and visibility.

- Social media sites- having a social media profile like Facebook, Twitter, that allows you to post content and share make you gain brand awareness and links back to your website, also you can obtain more online follower that spreading your website and brand virally through the web.

Overall, combining on- and off- page optimization will definitely help your business to maximize its visibility on search engines, as well as drive more traffic to your site through gained exposure of your brand online.

Tools and Application

Google Webmaster Tools

Google Webmasters is a free online tool and has been mentioned several times throughout this book. It is an extremely valuable tool for measuring and monitoring SEO progress. It will also help you to have a better understanding of your website's capabilities, competitors, and opportunities but that will require a lot of time to study and learn. This book will give you an initial guide to understand how to track and maintain your website, keeping search engines and customers happy. The following list below will give you how this tool can help you with your site.

•   It can see which web pages on your site are indexed with Google.

•   Has an ability to see errors encountered by Google when crawling your site.

- View all search engine queries that list or display you website as a result.
- You can also see all websites link to your website. (Incoming links)

Still the best way to learn about and understand how Google Webmasters work is to try it. A lot video tutorial has been uploaded on YouTube that can be served as your guide to learn and study Google Webmasters. Once you are done watching the tutorial you can follow these steps below to start.

1. Log in or create a Google Account.
2. Add your site to Google Webmaster Tools.
3. Verify your site with Google Webmaster Tools.
4. Lastly, submit a sitemap to Google Webmaster.

Keyword Density

https://www.webconfs.com/seo-tools/keyword-density-checker/ is one of the very effective tool to check your keyword density of your website. So that you can determine whether the web page is relevant to a specified keyword or phrase.

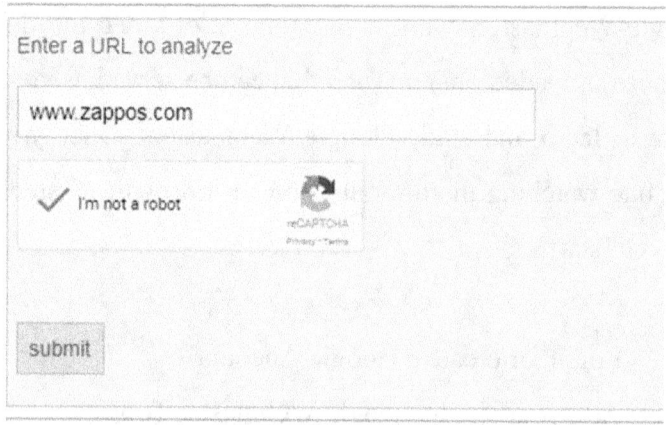

Keyword Density Checker

This tool will crawl the given URL, extract text as a search engine \
the keywords.

Enter a URL to analyze

www.zappos.com

✓ I'm not a robot

submit

Keyword Density

Keyword	Count	Density
zappos	14	2.36%
stars	11	1.85%
view	10	1.69%
ugg	10	1.69%
shoes	10	1.69%
ii	9	1.52%
boots	9	1.52%
shop	8	1.35%
classic	7	1.18%

The images above is an illustration how to use the tool and give you the result for keyword density of zappos.com

Keyword Research Tool

Here are some of the commonly used research tools for keywords.

• Google Insight tool – open source and valuable tool that enables you to search for keywords volume patterns based on geographical regions, timeframes and categories.,

• Google Search-based keyword tool provides keyword ideas based on the Google live search queries.

• Keyword Discover- collects keyword statistics from all major search engines while providing keyword density analysis. It is not an open source but there is a free-trial version.

Bonus Topic

Web Analytics

Web Analytics is the collective information of the measurement, collection, analysis and reporting of Internet data for the purpose of understanding and optimizing the web usage. Today, more and more marketers have discovered the value of online data. As web analytics evolve reports and online has become more sophisticated, refined and user-friendly. As marketers are now able to analyze the behavior of individual visitors, assess patterns and take action to improve sales and marketing initiatives. Understanding the psychology behind online behavior takes time, specialty, and lengthy data analysis and reporting.

As web analysis continue to evolve with innovative tools such as Crazy Egg (www.crazyegg.com), which uses heat maps to display the groups and density of clicks on a web page. And the Google entered the market introduced the Google Analytics (www.google.com/analytics), it is one of the most commonly used Web Analytics tool and a trendsetter with most of the marketers. Using Google Analytics provides a more engaging experience with real-time data, it will help you put in a good position to track trends and gain insight into your customer's online behavior. This tools module is all about how to start tracking your user behavior and what key statistics to focus on.

Benefits of web analytics

Before using any new tool, it is really important to understand first the value and outcomes. Here are the few benefits of web analytics.

- It can provide you key metrics and statistics of your visitors and users such as visits, unique visits, bounce rates, top content, top keywords that can you monitor their behaviors.
- Optimize your website, once you have identified and learned your user's behavior you will have a sufficient information to take actions/updates like changing the content of your landing pages, changing or adding to the navigations, add more calls to action on your homepage or even restricting URLs.
- Convey sales and internet marketing plan after analyzing the web data. From the key insights of your reports which can have a direct effect on marketing plans, it may help marketers leverage a

specific product or target a certain geographical location by analyzing the data to see the top traffic sources.

- Measure the profit contribution from online marketing initiatives. Using tools such as Google Analytics also enables you to create goals with specific values. Completing these goals helps your monitor a goal conversion and site optimization.

- Predict future trends. Once you see the trends from your customer's online behavior you will begin to ask yourself and check: when traffic to your site is high, which pages are more popular, what causes an increase in traffic and where the majority of visitors come from. These trends will help you predict future behavior that makes it easier to plan and execute future marketing campaigns based on the past results.

- Keep track of competition. Questions like how much traffic do they get? Where does the traffic come from and where is it going? First thing you have to do is take not of which competitor appear on the first page of search results and in sponsored links (paid-ad). You visit each competitor's website and view their source code. And from

47

there you will be able to see their meta-data and analyze to study your competitor's SEO strategy.

- Real-time data about online users. Being able to see the number of your visitors within seconds of sending out an email campaign or posting a viral video is invaluable information, this will help you to act and react in real time with your visitor.

- Monitor social media activity. Keeping up to date with social media activity with your customers such as quotable quotes, sharing and writing is one of the methods to build more engagement with your visitors. There are tools used to monitor visitors social media activity, these are saidWot (www.saidwot.com), trackur (www.trackur.com), Sentiment metric (www.sentimentmetrics.com) and Social mention (www.socialmention.com) are just a few examples. These tools will enable you to analyze key brand influences, manage your brand's online reputation and gain more insight into your customer's online activity.

Now that you understand what web analytics is and what the major benefits of it are, it is time to learn how to identify what parameters you need to measure and how to read analytics reports, set up conversion goals and gain valuable insights from data.

Track, Analyze, report

In order to analyze data, you first have to gather data. The first step to setting up any analytics tool is to generate a piece of JavaScript code and add it to all pages of your website. JavaScript is a special type of code that creates page tags and tracks data every time human clicks on a link that is connected to your website.

You must register in Google Analytics first in order to follow. First open a web browser, go to www.google.com/analytics and log in to your Google account. Once logged in, click on the "access analytics" button. You can also view these steps on a video tutorial online.

What parameters to measure?

The image below shows you an overview of Google Analytics interface that displays the most commonly parameters measured from the users online activity.

Country / Territory	Visits ↓	Pages / Visit	Avg. Visit Duration	% New Visits	Bounce Rate
	1,107,428 % of Total: 100.00% (1,107,476)	1.44 Site Avg: 1.44 (0.02%)	00:01:26 Site Avg: 00:01:26 (0.00%)	76.57% Site Avg: 76.47% (0.14%)	78.78% Site Avg: 78.78% (0.00%)
1. United States	513,945	1.40	00:01:15	77.42%	80.88%
2. India	90,278	1.74	00:02:38	74.33%	66.50%
3. United Kingdom	76,723	1.38	00:01:13	74.50%	80.88%
4. Canada	61,086	1.33	00:01:01	79.11%	82.12%
5. Philippines	31,315	1.63	00:02:31	72.13%	70.62%

Visits- are the number of unique sessions initiated by a reader. This statistic counts every time someone visits your site. If a visitor is inactive on your site for 30 minutes or more, it is counted as additional visits but not as an additional visitor

• Page views- the number of pages that were viewed during these visits. Page views are tracked by Google analytics. If a visitor hits reload after reaching a page, this will be counted as an additional page view. If a user navigates to a different page and then returns to the original page, this is counted as a page view as well.

- Unique page views- unique page views are therefore the number of sessions during which that page was viewed one or more times by the same visitor.

- Pages/visit- the average number of pages viewed during each visit.

- Bounce rate- the percentage of visits in which the person instantly leaves your site within seconds of arriving.

- Average time on site- the average length of time people stay on your site.

- Percentage of new visits- Percentage of people visiting your site for the first time.

- Top Content- a list of pages ranked by the amount of trafc they get. These are the key pages that you want to use to direct visitors to other pages on your site, as they get the most traffic.

Visitors

It is important to note that, depending on your industry, sales cycle and product, each statistic may have a unique significance. For example, take new versus returning visitors. If you are trying to build up a long-term relationship with customers and would like visitors to return to your site regularly, you will need to provide fresh content to encourage people to return and therefore returning visitors should be high. If you are selling something with a short sales cycle, you want visitors to land on your site and purchase something in the same session. If visitors cannot find what they are looking for in three clicks, they will be sure to click off your website

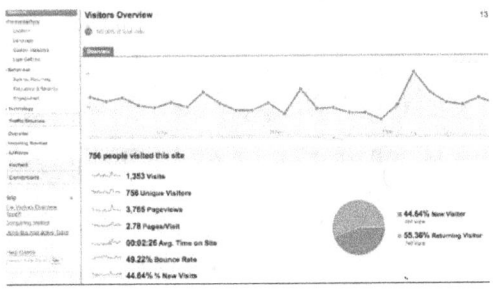

and not return.

Image above shows the visitor's statistics.

Key Visitors statistics:

• Absolute unique visitors- imagine you visit the same website three times in one week from the same computer using the same browser. You will be counted as one new unique visitor with three visits.

• Bounce rate- people who are clicking on your ad but will immediately leave if the site's content is not relevant to their search query.

• Benchmarking- Google has a new industry benchmarking tool. It assigns your site to an industry and then provides benchmark statistics. You are able to change the industry category list and compare you stats to multiple industries.

• Map overlay- the map overlay is very interesting as you can see where in the world the majority of your visitors come from. You can even filter by city, sub-continent region and continent.

Additional analytics tools:
We have now touched on some of the key principles, statistics and functionality
of web analytics, but there are still more interesting ways to analyze data and gain further customer insight which

will in turn boost your profits and aid in delivering more relevant content to your online customers.

This section explores additional research tools and desktop applications that can be used in conjunction with Google Analytics.

Woopra

A new competitor recently entered the market and has made quite a stir: Woopra (www.woopra.com), a real-time, desktop web analytics application. Do not compare Woopra with the market leading Google Analytics, but rather enjoy the benefit of both applications.

Differences between Google Analytics and Woopra:

Display - Woopra is a desktop application (you have to download a file to your computer) whereas Google Analytics is purely web based (accessible anywhere from any computer).

Registration- Woopra takes several days to approve your site registration. Google Analytics starts tracking data within 24 hours of adding tracking code to your site.

Real time- Woopra is a more attractive interface and data is displayed in real

Web analytics and conversion optimization time: it's instant. This does mean you're using more bandwidth and possibly that your website loading time will slow.

User interface- Woopra's interface is far less intimidating and more user friendly, but it does not have as many features as Google Analytics. Everything in Woopra is one click away, quick and simple.

Conversion goals- Google Analytics wins hands down here. Woopra does not have a goal function in their program.

Ecommerce and action- based reporting. Google Analytics has the ability to interface with AdWords and AdSense, show which pages are earning the most money and reveal what the expensive AdWords visitors are doing on your site. Woopra does not have this functionality.

In short, Woopra wins over Google Analytics for its interface's "wow" factor: it is simple to use and easy for beginners to really engage with their visitors and get excited about web analytics. Google Analytics is not real time but it does Web analytics and conversion have more bells and whistles, plus the integration with other Google services like AdWords. There is no one perfect web analytics tool; just remember that it's the insight you get from the data that is important – make sure you take action and don't just accumulate interesting statistics.

Summary

SEO

SEO is a gradual process that takes time, patience and a lot of research. Most sites will gain SEO traction gradually as they add new content to their site, tweak and optimize content over time and as search engines discover, index and understand their content, and as the amount of quality links pointing to their site increases. Always use ethical means to improve SEO and never take any technique to extreme measures as this may do your site more harm than good.

Web Analytics

Web analytics is not an option; it is requirement. All businesses, big or small, need some way to objectively track measure and analyze online user behavior in order to draw effective insights and optimize their websites, increase traffic, grow their customer databases and increase sales. The key to web analytics is first to define what you want to achieve. Make sure you have answered the following questions before you start signing up for multiple analytics tools.

Activity for Web Analytics before signing up to any analytic tool, make sure you answer all the questions below:

1.   What are your website conversion goals? Do you want your visitors to complete a contact form, download an information pack, buy a product, watch a promotional video or request more information?

2.   Have you mapped out the user journey for each goal? What is the ideal path a user should take to complete each goal? An online user sees a tweet about a competition to win a weekend away > clicks on the link which takes them to a competition entry page > submits the entry > arrives on a "thank you" page with a list of tours > clicks on a tour > views the tour detail page >

completes a "request for more information" form. The goal is complete.

3. Have you researched the competitiveness of keywords and their estimated traffic?

4. Have you completed on-page and off-page optimization?

5. What social media networks are you and your competitors using?

6. Have you set targets? What are your expected traffic, conversion rate, downloads, enquiries and sales? Web analytics and conversion optimization

In this book you:

Learned what SEO is and how search engines use this data to categorize your website.

Discovered that SEO is vital for ensuring that users and search engines can find your website easily.

Learned how to optimize your website for search engines by employing a range of techniques, from title tags to on-page copy.

Learned the best ways to optimize your website from off your page.

Discovered some useful tools for helping you optimize your website and improving the way search engines see your page.

Learn about search engines and how they interact with websites

Find out what search engine optimization (SEO) is

Discover why SEO is so important for your website

Learn how to optimize your website for search engines

Learn how to see what your competition is doing online

Learn about off-page optimization

Discover tools and applications that will help you optimize how search engines interact with your website

What Web Analytics is

Tools used to analyze customer online behavior

What Google Analytics is

Basics and Content Parameters need to learn in Google Analytics